This book is a gift to you from the American Poetry & Literacy Project, a nonprofit organization that distributes free books throughout the world to promote literacy and to foster a greater appreciation for poetry.

In partnership with the Olympics Arts Festival, Home Depot, and KaBOOM!, over 100,000 copies of this book are being distributed at the 2002 Olympic Winter Games in Salt Lake City. We hope you enjoy this collection of extraordinary poems from around the world and share it with others.

If you would like more information about the American Poetry & Literacy Project, please write to us at: PO Box 53445, Washington, DC 20009 USA. We'd like to hear from you.

# A World of Poetry

EDITED BY

## The American Poetry
## &
## Literacy Project

DOVER PUBLICATIONS, INC.
Mineola, New York

## Copyright

## Bibliographical Note

A *World of Poetry*, first published in 2002, is a new selection of poems published for
The American Poetry & Literacy Project by Dover Publications, Inc., Mineola, N.Y.

International Standard Book Number: 0-486-42208-9

Manufactured in the United States of America
Dover Publications, Inc., 31 East 2nd Street, Mineola, N.Y. 11501

# Table of Contents

### "The Happiness That Silent Keeps"
### Poems on Love & Friendship

### "A Single Shivering Fleck of Sunset-light"
### Poems on the Beauty of the World

### *"An Affirming Flame"*
### Poems on Peace & Hope

# INTRODUCTION

## Words of Gold

"POETRY," THE U.S. POET LAUREATE JOSEPH BRODSKY stated in a 1991 speech at the Library of Congress, "must be available to the public in far greater volume than it is."

When Brodsky went on to propose that anthologies of poetry be distributed freely in supermarkets and outside of assembly plants and factories, the audience burst into laughter. "At the very least," Brodsky maintained, "an anthology of poetry should be found in the drawer in every room in every motel in the land." Brodsky himself recognized how preposterous the idea must seem: "Even to sympathetic ears, I suppose, all this may sound a bit loony. Well, it isn't."

From this speech, the American Poetry & Literacy Project was born. Founded by Brodsky and a small cadre of volunteers in 1993, the APL Project has since given away almost one million free poetry books in public venues to people from all walks of life. Books have been distributed in hotels, jury waiting rooms, airplanes, trains, prisons, day-care centers, hospitals, subway stations, hotels, nursing homes, and truck stops. The APL Project has given away copies of Edgar Allan Poe's "The Raven" for Halloween and Spanish poetry for Cinco de Mayo. We have handed out Walt Whitman's "Leaves of Grass" from tollbooths at the Walt Whitman Bridge connecting New Jersey and Pennsylvania and offered anthologies of "Great Love Poems" in 24-hour wedding chapels in Las Vegas, Nevada.

We recognize that many people find poetry difficult and obscure. Even the famed writer Marianne Moore, in a poem entitled "Poetry," famously exclaimed: "I, too, dislike it: there are things that are important beyond all this fiddle." In fact, those who have no interest in poetry are the very ones we strive to reach. The purpose of our give-aways is to surprise people who might not otherwise pick up a collection of verse, and remind them of all that poetry has to offer. We believe that poetry is not a luxury for the few, but a necessity for all. Some turn to poetry for solace or hope. Others look for wisdom. And some simply enjoy the sound and rhythm of the words. Marianne Moore later conceded that she found poetry not entirely without merit: "Reading it, however, with a perfect contempt for it, one discovers in it after all, a place for the genuine." Poetry is about the genuine, about truth. It is about passion and love, wonder and creativity, empathy and perseverance. In short, it encompasses everything that makes life worthwhile.

A *World of Poetry* was created specifically for the 2002 Olympic Winter Games in Salt Lake City, Utah, and it is the first international anthology of poems the American Poetry & Literacy Project has edited. Sixty poets from almost 40 countries are featured in this collection, spanning over 2,500 years of human history. Whether they were penned by a Persian poet from the 10th century or a Polish writer from the 21st, these poems are remarkable not for their differences in themes and emotions, but for their striking similarities: Regardless of geography or era, they all express a profound appreciation for the world's astonishing beauty, a recognition of love's ability to infuse life with joy and meaning, a yearning for peace, and a call for courage and compassion. They are sentiments that know no borders and resonate throughout the ages.

They remind us as well that just as there is a lyricism and grace to athletics, there is energy and power to poetry. The poets featured here celebrate human ideals as triumphantly as those who distinguish themselves on the fields and in the stadiums of the Olympic Games. They, too, are testaments to stamina and discipline. They, too, demonstrate agility and swiftness. Their work may be done in private, far from cheering crowds, but their achievements also challenge and inspire the world. Like the Olympic Games themselves, these poets represent a gathering of hearts and minds, impassioned, strong, and indomitable. They celebrate what is best and most noble about humanity. They celebrate us all.

# A World of Poetry

Water is preeminent and gold, like a fire
        burning in the night, outshines
all possessions that magnify men's pride.
        But if, my soul, you yearn
            to celebrate great games,
                look no further
                for another star
            shining through the deserted ether
    brighter than the sun, or for a contest
mightier than Olympia—

                —From *Olympian Ode 1*
    by Pindar (Greece; 518 B.C.E.–c. 438 B.C.E.)

## *"Of Gold and Glory"*
## Poems on Competing, Playing & Persevering

### *From* To Chaadaev
Aleksandr Pushkin
*(Russia; 1799–1837)*

Our dreams of love and modest glory,
delusive hopes now quickly sped,
our pranks and games, our youth's brief story
like sleep or morning mist are fled;
and yet, within, desires still quicken,
our souls impatient for their hour,
while yoked beneath a fateful power
our country calls to us, heart-stricken.
We wait now, wearied-out with yearning
lest sacred freedom come too late,
as some young lover, too, might wait
the tryst for which his heart is burning.
So while for freedom's flame we live
and honor in our breast we treasure,
friend, let us to our homeland give
the noblest that our souls can measure.

### Skier
Robert Francis
*(United States of America; 1901–1987)*

He swings down like the flourish of a pen
Signing a signature in white on white.

The silence of his skis reciprocates
The silence of the world around him.

Wind is his one competitor
In the cool winding and unwinding down.

On incandescent feet he falls
Unfalling, trailing white foam, white fire.

3

## The Acrobat
### Wisława Szymborska
### *(Poland; 1923–        )*

From trapczc to
to trapeze, in the hush that
that follows the drum roll's sudden pause, through
through the startled air, more swiftly than
than his body's weight, which once again
again is late for its own fall.

Solo. Or even less than solo,
less, because he's crippled, missing
missing wings, missing them so much
that he can't miss the chance
to soar on shamefully unfeathered
naked vigilance alone.

Arduous ease,
watchful agility,
and calculated inspiration. Do you see
how he waits to pounce in flight; do you know
how he plots from head to toe
against his very being; do you know, do you see
how cunningly he weaves himself through his own former shape
and works to seize this swaying world
by stretching out the arms he has conceived—

beautiful beyond belief at this passing
at this very passing moment that's just passed.

## First Love
Carl Lindner
*(United States of America; 1940–          )*

Before sixteen
I was fast
enough to fake
my shadow out
and I could read
every crack and ripple
in that catch of asphalt.
I owned
the slanted rim
knew
the dead spot in the backboard.
Always the ball
came back.

Every day I loved
to sharpen
my shooting eye,
waiting
for the touch.
Set shot, jump shot,
layup, hook—
after a while
I could feel
the ball hunger-
ing to clear
the lip of the rim,
the two of us
falling through.

## Baseball
Linda Pastan
*(United States of America; 1932–          )*

When you tried to tell me
baseball was a metaphor

for life: the long, dusty travail
around the bases, for instance,

to try to go home again;
the Sacrifice for which you win

approval but not applause;
the way the light closes down

in the last days of the season—
I didn't believe you.

It's just a way of passing
the time, I said.

And you said: that's it.
Yes.

# The Jogger on Riverside Drive, 5:00 A.M.
## Agha Shahid Ali
### *(Kashmir/United States of America; 1949–      )*

The dark scissors of his legs
cut the moon's

raw silk, highways of wind
torn into lanes, his feet

pushing down the shadow
whose patterns he becomes

while trucks, one by one,
pass him by,

headlights pouring
from his face, his eyes

cracked as the Hudson
wraps street lamps

in its rippled blue shells,
the summer's thin, thin veins

bursting with dawn,
he, now suddenly free,

from the air, from himself,
his heart beating far, far

behind him.

## Competition
### Stephen Dunn
*(United States of America; 1939–        )*

Because he played games seriously
    and therefore knew grace
comes hard, rises through the cheap

in us, the petty, the entire history
    of our defeats,
he looked for grace in his opponents,

found a few friends that way
    and so many others
he could never drink with, talk to.

He learned early never to let up,
    never to give
a weaker opponent a gift

because so many times he'd been
    that person
and knew the humiliation in it,

being pandered to, a bone for the sad
    dog.
And because he remembered those times

after a loss when he'd failed
    at grace—
stole from the victor

the pleasures of pure victory
    by speaking
about a small injury or the cold

he wasn't quite over—he loved
    those opponents
who'd shake hands and give credit,

save their true and bitter stories
    for their lovers, later,
when all such lamentations are comic,

the sincere *if onlys* of grown men
    in short pants.
Oh there were people who thought

all of it so childish; what to say
    to them, how to agree,
ever, about dignity and fairness?


### One Art
Elizabeth Bishop
*(United States of America; 1911–1979)*

The art of losing isn't hard to master;
so many things seem filled with the intent
to be lost that their loss is no disaster.

Lose something every day. Accept the fluster
of lost door keys, the hour badly spent.
The art of losing isn't hard to master.

Then practice losing farther, losing faster:
places, and names, and where it was you meant
to travel. None of these will bring disaster.

I lost my mother's watch. And look! my last, or
next-to-last, of three loved houses went.
The art of losing isn't hard to master.

I lost two cities, lovely ones. And, vaster,
some realms I owned, two rivers, a continent.
I miss them, but it wasn't a disaster.

—Even losing you (the joking voice, a gesture
I love) I shan't have lied. It's evident
the art of losing's not too hard to master
though it may look like (*Write* it!) like disaster.

## Blacksmith Pain
Otto Julius Bierbaum
*(Germany; 1865–1910)*

Pain is a blacksmith,
Hard is his hammer;
With flying flames
His hearth is hot;
A straining storm
Of forces ferocious
Blows his bellows.
He hammers hearts
And tinkers them,
With blows tremendous,
Till hard they hold.—
Well, well forges Pain.—
No storm destroys,
No frost consumes,
No rust corrodes,
What Pain has forged.

## "I Think Over Again My Small Adventures"
Anonymous
*(North American Indian; 19th century)*

I think over again my small adventures,
My fears,
Those small ones that seemed so big,
For all the vital things
I had to get and to reach;
And yet there is only one great thing,
The only thing,
To live to see the great day that dawns
And the light that fills the world.

### *From* I Am a Black Woman
Mari Evans
*(United States of America; 1923–      )*

> I
> am a black woman
> tall as a cypress
> strong
> beyond all definition still
> defying place
> and time
> and circumstance
>    assailed
>       impervious
>          indestructible
> Look
>    on me and be
> renewed


### "Just as a Flame, by Wind and Weather Flailed"
Michelangelo Buonarroti
*(Italy; 1475–1564)*

Just as a flame, by wind and weather flailed,
flares up, so every virtue prized by heaven
is more resplendent, being more assailed.

# I Also Sing of Myself
### Soleida Ríos
*(Cuba; 1950–        )*

> *I celebrate myself, I sing*
> *—Walt Whitman*

I sing of myself because by force of love
I stand,
squeezing this curve of time
between my hands.

The morning stretches out over silence
and my steps
call back the high sounds.

I sing of myself and beyond, I sing
of what I will become
when night is rent by sun
and another music fills my footprints as I go.

I sing of myself
for having come from the breath of a summer
among these palms that will watch over me
I take my place among the living
I make infinite my thirst
striking myself, I sing.

## The Way of the Water-Hyacinth
### Zawgee
### *(Burma; 1907–1990)*

Bobbing on the breeze blown waves
Bowing to the tide
Hyacinth rises and falls

Falling but not felled
By flotsam, twigs, leaves
She ducks, bobs and weaves.

Ducks, ducks by the score
Jolting, quacking and more
She spins through—

Spinning, swamped, slimed, sunk
She rises, resolute
Still crowned by petals.


## Sunset
### Rainer Maria Rilke
### *(Austria; 1875–1926)*

Slowly the west reaches for clothes of new colors
which it passes to a row of ancient trees.
You look, and soon these two worlds both leave you,
one part climbs toward heaven, one sinks to earth,

leaving you, not really belonging to either,
not so hopelessly dark as that house that is silent,
not so unswervingly given to the eternal as that thing
that turns to a star each night and climbs—

leaving you (it is impossible to untangle the threads)
your own life, timid and standing high and growing,
so that, sometimes blocked in, sometimes reaching out,
one moment your life is a stone in you, and the next, a star.

# To an Athlete Dying Young
### A.E. Housman
### (Great Britain; 1859–1936)

The time you won your town the race
We chaired you through the market-place;
Man and boy stood cheering by,
And home we brought you shoulder-high.

To-day, the road all runners come,
Shoulder-high we bring you home,
And set you at your threshold down,
Townsman of a stiller town.

Smart lad, to slip betimes away
From fields where glory does not stay
And early though the laurel grows
It withers quicker than the rose.

Eyes the shady night has shut
Cannot see the record cut,
And silence sounds no worse than cheers
After earth has stopped the ears:

Now you will not swell the rout
Of lads that wore their honours out,
Runners whom renown outran
And the name died before the man.

So set, before its echoes fade,
The fleet foot on the sill of shade,
And hold to the low lintel up
The still-defended challenge-cup.

And round that early-laurelled head
Will flock to gaze the strengthless dead,
And find unwithered on its curls
The garland briefer than a girl's.

### *From* **Muhammad Ali at the Ringside, 1985**
Wole Soyinka
*(Nigeria; 1934–     )*

Cassius Marcellus, Warrior, Muhammad Prophet,
Flesh is clay, all, all too brittle mould.
The bout is over. Frayed and split and autographed,
The gloves are hung up in the Hall of Fame—
Still loaded, even from that first blaze of gold
And glory. Awed multitudes will gaze,
New questers feast on these mementos
And from their shell-shocked remnants
Reinvoke the spell. But the sorcerer is gone,
The lion withdrawn to a lair of time and space
Inaccessible as the sacred lining of a crown
When kings were kings, and lords of rhyme and pace.
The enchantment is over but the spell remains.

*"The Happiness That Silent Keeps"*
Poems on Love & Friendship

### Sonnet XXX
William Shakespeare
*(Great Britain; 1564–1616)*

When to the sessions of sweet silent thought
I summon up remembrance of things past,
I sigh the lack of many a thing I sought,
And with old woes new wail my dear times' waste:
Then can I drown an eye, unus'd to flow,
For precious friends hid in death's dateless night,
And weep afresh love's long since cancell'd woe,
And moan the expense of many a vanish'd sight:
Then can I grieve at grievances foregone,
And heavily from woe to woe tell o'er
The sad account of fore-bemoaned moan,
Which I new pay as if not paid before.
  But if the while I think on thee, dear friend,
  All losses are restor'd and sorrows end.

### *From* Sonnet XVII
Pablo Neruda
*(Chile; 1904–1973)*

I love you without knowing how, or when, or from where,
I love you simply, without problems or pride:
I love you in this way because I don't know any other way of
    loving

but this, in which there is no I or you,
so intimate that your hand upon my chest is my hand,
so intimate that when I fall asleep it is your eyes that close.


### On the River Tchou
Tu Fu
*(China; 712–770)*

My boat glides swiftly
beneath the wide cloud-ridden sky,
and as I look into the river
I can see the clouds drift by the moon;
my boat seems floating
on the sky.

And thus I dream
my beloved is mirrored
on my heart.

# A Song
## Joseph Brodsky
### (Russia; 1940–1996)

I wish you were here, dear,
I wish you were here.
I wish you sat on the sofa
and I sat near.
The handkerchief could be yours,
the tear could be mine, chin-bound.
Though it could be, of course,
the other way around.

I wish you were here, dear,
I wish you were here.
I wish we were in my car,
and you'd shift the gear.
We'd find ourselves elsewhere,
on an unknown shore.
Or else we'd repair
to where we've been before.

I wish you were here, dear,
I wish you were here.
I wish I knew no astronomy
when stars appear,
when the moon skims the water
that sighs and shifts in its slumber.
I wish it were still a quarter
to dial your number.

I wish you were here, dear,
in this hemisphere,
as I sit on the porch
sipping a beer.
It's evening, the sun is setting;
boys shout and gulls are crying.
What's the point of forgetting
if it's followed by dying?

### O, Keep Quiet. . . .
Matilda Cugler-Poni
*(Romania; 1851–1931)*

O, keep quiet and let time elapse
Like the water that flows in the valley,
Both mirroring all on its shores
And never suspending its course.

Let my head find its rest
On your chest, in sweet peace,
For the greatest of all happiness
Is the happiness that silent keeps.

### Kisses
Rudaki
*(Persia; 10th century)*

Kisses are like salt water,
The more you drink, the more you thirst.

### The Footsteps
Paul Valéry
*(France; 1871–1945)*

Your footsteps, born of my silence,
With a slow and saintly pace,
Approach the bed from where I
Watch, quiet and still.

Pure one, divine of spirit,
How gentle are your cautious steps!
Gods! . . . all that life could offer
Comes to me on those bare feet!

If, with your lips advancing,
You are preparing to appease
The inhabitant of these thoughts
With the nourishment of a kiss,

Do not hurry this tender act,
Sweetness full and incomplete,
For I have lived awaiting you,
Your footfall was my own heart's beat.


### *From* Hold
Yu Kuang-chung
*(Taiwan; 1928–    )*

I still hold your hand, a frightened starling—
Too tight, I fear stifling it;
too loose,
it might take wing.

## Song for the Goddess of Love
Sappho
*(Greece; 7th century* B.C.E.*)*

Leave Crete,
Aphrodite,
and come to this
sacred place
encircled by apple trees,
fragrant with offered smoke.

Here, cold springs
sing softly
amid the branches;
the ground is shady with roses;
from trembling young leaves
a deep drowsiness pours.

In the meadow,
horses are cropping the wildflowers of spring,
scented fennel
blows on the breeze.

In this place,
Lady of Cyprus, pour
the nectar that honors you
into our cups,
gold, and raised for the drinking.

## Walking Westward in the Morning
Sapardi Djoko Damono
(*Indonesia; 1940–     *)

walking westward in the morning the sun follows from behind
I walk following my lengthened shadow before me
the sun and I don't argue about which one of us creates the
     shadow
the shadow and I don't argue about which one of us must lead
     the way

## My Mind
Tongmyong Kim
(*Korea; 1901–1966*)

My mind is a lake;
come and row your boat in it.
I will hug your white shadow
and break into jewels against your sides.

My mind is a candlelight;
please close the window for me.
I will burn myself, quiet, to the last drop
trembling by your silken dress.

My mind is a wanderer;
play on your flute for me.
I will stay the quiet night through
listening to your tunes under the moon.

My mind is a falling leaf;
let me stay in your garden awhile.
I will leave you as a lonely wanderer
when the wind rises again.

### Presence
Ali al-Sharqawi
*(Bahrain; 1948–          )*

At night's end you arrive,
a bird chosen by morning,
alighting on my shoulder,
and I sprout leaves like lightning
amidst these winds.
They redden like a promise before it ripens,
broaching the thought of departing from worry to dream.
Laughter of lighthouses echoes
across the spacious darkness.
You arrive like sails
journeying across my lips.
As distance expands with you,
I expand.
Your mast extends across the day.
I am a bud seamed by a country
where wishes blaze and songs collapse the walls.
You are the gem of my soul,
clarity of love that shimmers in palm trees.
You arrive in everything,
the words passed from bird to prisoned bird,
the wind's child migrating from one homeland to another,
the dream, venturing into untracked territory—
In everything you come,
the radiant foliage of the spirit
embracing the feast of seasons,
the bride's passion as she hangs up
    her wedding dress.
You arrive—it is enough
    that your presence is a sea,
        my heart is a sail,
            and there is no coastline.

### Confession
Bub Bridger
*(New Zealand; 1924–      )*

I'm a little in love with you
Nothing
To cause you embarrassment
Or concern
Just a warm
Skip of the heart
When I see you from
My bus
At your stop

I catch your eye
And give you a wave
And I note
That you are more beautiful
Now than you ever were
And I am a keen
Observer of beauty
Whether it's sunsets
Or music
Or the Mona Lisa
Or birds flying
Or green growing things
Or you

So
How does it feel
My young Adonis to be
Held in such regard
By an elderly lady
On the 24 Express?
Well

Don't knock it
Because it really is
A rare compliment
And you
Only have to respond
With your wide smile
Which is a small price
To pay
For allowing me my glimpse
Of what it used to be
All those years ago
When I was seventeen
And beautiful young men
Smiled
By the dozen

## Two Bodies
Octavio Paz
*(Mexico; 1914–1998)*

Two bodies face to face
are at times two waves
and night is an ocean.

Two bodies face to face
are at times two stones
and night a desert.

Two bodies face to face
are at times two roots
laced into night.

Two bodies face to face
are at times two knives
and night strikes sparks.

Two bodies face to face
are two stars falling
in an empty sky.

## The Song of Wandering Aengus
### William Butler Yeats
### *(Ireland; 1865–1939)*

I went out to the hazel wood,
Because a fire was in my head,
And cut and peeled a hazel wand,
And hooked a berry to a thread;
And when white moths were on the wing,
And moth-like stars were flickering out,
I dropped the berry in a stream
And caught a little silver trout.

When I had laid it on the floor
I went to blow the fire aflame,
But something rustled on the floor,
And some one called me by my name:
It had become a glimmering girl
With apple blossoms in her hair
Who called me by my name and ran
And faded through the brightening air.

Though I am old with wandering
Through hollow lands and hilly lands,
I will find out where she has gone,
And kiss her lips and take her hands;
And walk among long dappled grass,
And pluck till time and times are done
The silver apples of the moon,
The golden apples of the sun.

## "A Single Shivering Fleck of Sunset-light"
## Poems on the Beauty of the World

## On the Mountain:
## A Conversation
Li Po
*(China; 701–762)*

you ask
why I perch
on a jade green mountain?
I laugh
but say nothing
my heart
free
like a peach blossom
in the flowing stream
going by
in the depths
in another world
not among men


## A Woman Shaman's Song
Uvavnuk
*(Canada/Iglulik Eskimo; 19th century)*

The great sea stirs me.
The great sea sets me free,
Sways me like a weed
On a river stone.

The great sky stirs me.
The strong wind moves me,
Carries me away
And fills my soul with joy.

# All That You Have Given Me, Africa
## Anoma Kanié
### *(Ivory Coast; 20th century)*

All that you have given me, Africa
Lakes, forests, misted lagoons
All that you have given me,
Music, dances, all night stories around a fire
All that you have etched in my skin
Pigments of my ancestors
Indelible in my blood
All that you have given me Africa
Makes me walk
With a step that is like no other
Hip broken under the weight of time,
Feet large with journeys,
All that you have left to me
Even this lassitude bound to my heels,
I bear it with pride on my forehead
My health is no more to be lost
And I go forward
Praising my race which is no better
Or worse than any other.
All that you have given me Africa,
Savannahs gold in the noonday sun
Your beasts that men call wicked,
Your mines, inexplicable treasures
Obsession of a hostile world
Your suffering for lost paradises,
All that, I protect with an unforgiving hand
As far as the clear horizons
So that your heaven-given task
May be safe forever.

### Sung
#### Gunnar Ekelöf
#### *(Sweden; 1907–1968)*

The stars are clear tonight.
The air is pure and cold.
The moon is looking for her lost
inheritance everywhere.

A window, a branch in blossom
and that is enough:
No blossom without earth.
No earth without space.
No space without blossom.


### Childhood Morning—Homebush
#### James McAuley
#### *(Australia; 1917–1976)*

The half-moon is a muted lamp
Motionless behind a veil.
As the eastern sky grows pale,
I hear the slow-train's puffing stamp

Gathering speed. A bulbul sings,
Raiding persimmon and fig.
The rooster in full glossy rig
Crows triumph at the state of things.

I make no comment; I don't know;
I hear that every answer's No,
But can't believe it can be so.

### *From* Gift
Rabindranath Tagore
*(India; 1861–1941)*

O my love, what gift of mine
   Shall I give you this dawn?
      A morning song?
   But morning does not last long—
     The heat of the sun
       Wilts it like a flower
     And songs that tire
       Are done.

O friend, when you come to my gate
     At dusk
   What is it you ask?
     What shall I bring you?
       A light?
  A lamp from a secret corner of my silent house?
    But will you want to take it with you
      Down the crowded street?
      Alas,
    The wind will blow it out.

Whatever gifts are in my power to give you,
    Be they flowers,
   Be they gems for your neck,
      How can they please you
     If in time they must surely wither,
      Crack,
       Lose lustre?
  All that my hands can place in yours
    Will slip through your fingers
      And fall forgotten to the dust
       To turn into dust.

Rather,
When you have leisure,
Wander idly through my garden in spring
And let an unknown, hidden flower's scent startle you
Into sudden wondering—
Let that displaced moment
Be my gift.
Or if, as you peer your way down a shady avenue,
Suddenly, spilled
From the thick gathered tresses of evening
A single shivering fleck of sunset-light stops you,
Turns your daydreams to gold,
Let that light be an innocent
Gift.

Truest treasure is fleeting;
It sparkles for a moment, then goes.
It does not tell its name; its tune
Stops us in our tracks, its dance disappears
At the toss of an anklet.
I know no way to it—
No hand, nor word can reach it.
Friend, whatever you take of it,
On your own,
Without asking, without knowing, let that
Be yours.

# FOUR SEASONS OF HAIKUS

### Summer
Kawabata Bōsha
*(Japan; 1900–1941)*

Fireflies at nightfall—
a chain of bright beads
along the water's edge.

### Autumn
Arakida Moritake
*(Japan; 1473–1549)*

A colorful falling leaf
drifts to a branch—
No, a butterfly!

### Winter
Takarai Kikaku
*(Japan; 1661–1707)*

The cold moon shines
on the matting on the floor,
thin shadows of the pines.

## Spring
Matsuo Bashō
*(Japan; 1644–1694)*

The temple bell stops,
but the ringing echoes
From out of the blossoms.


## The Negro Speaks of Rivers
Langston Hughes
*(United States of America; 1902–1967)*

I've known rivers:
I've known rivers ancient as the world and older than the
    flow of human blood in human veins.

My soul has grown deep like the rivers.

I bathed in the Euphrates when dawns were young.
I built my hut near the Congo and it lulled me to sleep.
I looked upon the Nile and raised the pyramids above it.
I heard the singing of the Mississippi when Abe Lincoln
    went down to New Orleans, and I've seen its muddy
    bosom turn all golden in the sunset.

I've known rivers:
Ancient, dusky rivers.

My soul has grown deep like the rivers.

## Native
Valerie Gillies
*(Scotland; 1948–     )*

The first stir of a southern autumn
And how I missed Scotland;
A restlessness for those quiet purples begun
When my eyes wanted all light shunned

Save that shining from the skies' grace
Upon our own homeland, the heart's place;
I am to my country
A leaf on which the likeness of the tree is traced.


## Snowfall
Mark Strand
*(United States of America; 1934–     )*

Watching snow cover the ground, cover itself,
cover everything that is not you, you see
it is the downward drift of light
upon the sound of air sweeping away the air,
it is the fall of moments into moments, the burial
of sleep, the down of winter, the negative of night.

## Ama Credo
Margaret Reckord Bernal
*(Jamaica; 1946–     )*

Needing
to go separate
along my green homings
barefoot to the thud
of fruit falling
solitaire calling
my compass, lodestar
glinting upmountain
hemmed in with pineneedles
canopied with sunsets
flaming me steeds
to stride
across sky on;
world softening
to mist
mornings shaking open
blue tablecloths
for me
to write big
and brief
on.

# The Infinite
Giacomo Leopardi
*(Italy; 1798–1837)*

I have always loved this lonely hill,
This hedge as well, although it veils
So large a view of the far-flung horizon.
And sitting here, lost in thought,
I envision a space beyond what I have known,
Of endless silence and a calm so eternal
It brings the heart near to terror.
Then as I hear the wind among the leaves,
I consider this sound against that eternity,
The breathing, vivid present against the infinite;
In such immensity my spirit drowns,
And sweet to me is shipwreck in this sea.

*"An Affirming Flame"*
Poems on Peace & Hope

## "Today, Like Every Other Day"
### Jalal al-din Rumi
#### *(Afghanistan/Turkey; 1207–1273)*

Today, like every other day, we wake up empty
and frightened. Don't open the door to the study
and begin reading. Take down a musical instrument.

Let the beauty we love be what we do.
There are hundreds of ways to kneel and kiss the ground.


## "Hope Is the Thing with Feathers"
### Emily Dickinson
#### *(United States of America; 1830–1886)*

Hope is the thing with feathers
That perches in the soul,
And sings the tune without the words,
And never stops at all,

And sweetest in the gale is heard;
And sore must be the storm
That could abash the little bird
That kept so many warm.

I've heard it in the chillest land,
And on the strangest sea;
Yet, never, in extremity,
It asked a crumb of me.

## First Day After the War
Mazisi Kunene
*(South Africa; 1930–      )*

We heard the songs of a wedding party.
We saw a soft light
Coiling round the young blades of grass
At first we hesitated, then we saw her footprints,
Her face emerged, then her eyes of freedom!
She woke us up with a smile saying,
"What day is this that comes suddenly?"
We said, "It is the first day after the war."
Then without waiting we ran to the open space
Ululating to the mountains and the pathways
Calling people from all the circles of the earth.
We shook up the old man demanding a festival
We asked for all the first fruits of the season.
We held hands with a stranger
We shouted across the waterfalls
People came from all lands
It was the first day of peace.
We saw our Ancestors travelling tall on the horizon.

## *From* Peace
Bakchylides
*(Greece; 5th century B.C.E.)*

In the iron-covered shield
the brown spider hangs his web.
The sharpened spear and double-edge sword
are flaked with rust.
The noise of the brass trumpet is dead,
and the honey of our dawnsleep
is not dried from our eyelids.
Streets clamor with happy outdoor banquets,
and the lovely hymns sung by children
spring like fire up into the bright air.

## An Appendix to the Vision of Peace
### Yehuda Amichai
*(Israel; 1924–2000)*

Don't stop after beating the swords
into ploughshares, don't stop! Go on beating
and make musical instruments out of them.

Whoever wants to make war again
will have to turn them into ploughshares first.

## *From* Letters to Childhood
### Mohammed Shehadeh
*(Palestinian; 20th/21st century)*

All the children of the world,
in all my abodes
you are the roses in my courtyard,
the green and the fresh,
the sun and the stars,
you are the beautiful hands,
the ones who raise the flag of childhood high.

I give my life to you.
To you I write my poems.

### Working Together
David Whyte
*(Great Britain/Ireland/*
*United States of America, 1955–   )*

We shape our self
to fit this world

and by the world
are shaped again.

The visible
and the invisible

working together
in common cause,

to produce
the miraculous.

I am thinking of the way
the intangible air

passed at speed
round a shaped wing

easily
holds our weight.

So may we, in this life
trust

to those elements
we have yet to see

or imagine,
and look for the true

shape of our own self,
by forming it well

to the great
intangibles about us.

## Fire in the Wood
### Ngo Chan Luu
*(Vietnam; 19th century)*

The wood has fire in it.
It has just come back to life.
Can you argue that wood has no fire in it
When rubbing brings out these flames?

## Poem Written in a Copy of *Beowulf*
### Jorge Luis Borges
*(Argentina; 1899–1986)*

At various times, I have asked myself what reasons
moved me to study, while my night came down,
without particular hope of satisfaction,
the language of the blunt-tongued Anglo-Saxons.

Used up by the years, my memory
loses its grip on words that I have vainly
repeated and repeated. My life in the same way
weaves and unweaves its weary history.

Then I tell myself: it must be that the soul
has some secret, sufficient way of knowing
that it is immortal, that its vast, encompassing
circle can take in all, can accomplish all.

Beyond my anxiety, beyond this writing,
the universe waits, inexhaustible, inviting.

## Try to Praise the Mutilated World
Adam Zagajewski
*(Poland; 1945–        )*

Try to praise the mutilated world.
Remember June's long days,
and wild strawberries, drops of wine, the dew.
The nettles that methodically overgrow
the abandoned homesteads of exiles.
You must praise the mutilated world.
You watched the stylish yachts and ships;
one of them had a long trip ahead of it,
while salty oblivion awaited others.
You've seen the refugees heading nowhere,
you've heard the executioners sing joyfully.
You should praise the mutilated world.
Remember the moments when we were together
in a white room and the curtain fluttered.
Return in thought to the concert where music flared.
You gathered acorns in the park in autumn
and leaves eddied over the earth's scars.
Praise the mutilated world
and the gray feather a thrush lost,
and the gentle light that strays and vanishes
and returns.

### *From* September 1, 1939
W.H. Auden
*(Great Britain; 1907–1973)*

Defenceless under the night
Our world in stupor lies;
Yet, dotted everywhere,
Ironic points of light
Flash out wherever the Just
Exchange their messages:
May I, composed like them
Of Eros and of dust,
Beleaguered by the same
Negation and despair,
Show an affirming flame.

### Quintrain
Sa´id ´Aql
*(Lebanon; 1912–        )*

Once . . . I heard a bird,
an absorbed, ecstatic bird,
eloquently telling
its child:
"Fly away,
soar high:
a few bread crumbs
will suffice you,
but the sky
you need . . .
the whole sky."

# Miracles
## Walt Whitman
### *(United States of America; 1819–1892)*

Why, who makes much of a miracle?
As to me I know of nothing else but miracles,
Whether I walk the streets of Manhattan,
Or dart my sight over the roofs of houses toward the sky,
Or wade with naked feet along the beach just in the edge of the
    water,
Or stand under trees in the woods,
Or talk by day with any one I love, or sleep in the bed at night
    with any one I love,
Or sit at table at dinner with the rest,
Or look at strangers opposite me riding in the car,
Or watch honey-bees busy around the hive of a summer
    forenoon,
Or animals feeding in the fields,
Or birds, or the wonderfulness of insects in the air,
Or the wonderfulness of the sundown, or of stars shining so
    quiet and bright,
Or the exquisite delicate thin curve of the new moon in spring;
These with the rest, one and all, are to me miracles,
The whole referring, yet each distinct and in its place.

To me every hour of the light and dark is a miracle,
Every cubic inch of space is a miracle,
Every square yard of the surface of the earth is spread with the
    same,
Every foot of the interior swarms with the same.

To me the sea is a continual miracle,
The fishes that swim—the rocks—the motion of the waves—
    the ships with men in them,
What stranger miracles are there?

## *From* "Tell Me, Do You Remember. . . ."
### Pedro Salinas
### *(Spain; 1892–1951)*

Tell me, do you remember
the dreams when they were there
before us?
How far away they seemed
from the eyes.
They resembled high clouds,
floating phantoms,
ever receding horizons.
Now gaze on them with me,
they are behind us.
If they were remote horizons,
to see them now
we must turn our heads
for we are far beyond them.
We are on the other side
of the dreams that we dreamed,
And we two need only gaze
in the distance, at the clouds,
to find other new ones
that urge fresh life upon us.
Gazing at us, face to face,
seeing us in that which we did,
there springs up,
from joys already fulfilled,
the happiness of the future
calling to us.

## Alphabetical List of Titles

# Alphabetical List of Poets

# Acknowledgments

First and foremost, on behalf of the American Poetry & Literacy Project, I would like to thank Mary Yelanjian, associate artistic director of the 2002 Olympic Winter Games. Mary approached us in February 1999 with the idea of doing an international collection of poetry, and it has been a joy and a pleasure working with her and her colleagues Eugenie Hero and Jim Glenn these past few years.

I am indebted to Darell Hammond, who is the founder of what I believe to be one of the greatest nonprofit organizations ever created—KaBOOM!, which works with communities throughout the United States and even in other countries to build playgrounds for children. Darell was instrumental in helping us secure funding for this book from Home Depot, and his extraordinary assistant, Gayle C. Todd, typed all the poems. Jonathan Roseman and Pat Chandler, at Home Depot, are responsible for helping us fund this book, and I am especially grateful to them.

I am also grateful to Clarence Strowbridge, M.C. Waldrep, Irene Kupferman, and Frank Fontana at Dover Publications for formatting and printing this book. The APL Project has worked for almost ten years with Dover, and thanks to them we have been able to distribute hundreds of thousands of free poetry books nationwide. I would also like to extend a special thanks to Paul Klein. If it were not for Paul, the APL Project simply would not be able to do what it strives to do.

I am indebted to Robbie Klein, my coeditor for this book, who spent hours upon hours seeking out poems from around the world. Robbie found some of the best poems in the collection, and she proofread the final draft.

For their assistance in recommending poems and helping in

other important ways, I am extremely grateful to: Mary
Esselman, CR Hibbs, Jake Jeppson, Lucas Klein, Chrissy Kolaya,
Estelle Lynch, Allen Mikaelian, Brook Miller, Naomi Shihab
Nye, Shana and Craig Shontz, Elizabeth Velez, and Ellen
Wingard.

I cannot thank Fred Courtright and Cathy Gruber enough for
all their help with getting permission to use the poems in this
collection.

Finally, I would like to thank the APL Project's board of di-
rectors: Sue Halpern, Edward Hirsch, Sunil Iyengar, Henry
Labalme, Josie Merck, John Noonan, Elizabeth Elam Roth, and
Betsy Taylor. Their support and guidance have been invaluable.

                    —Andrew Carroll
                     Executive Director,
                     The American Poetry & Literacy Project

## Permissions